YOUR KNOWLEDG

G000141172

- We will publish your bachelor's and master's thesis, essays and papers

- Your own eBook and book - sold worldwide in all relevant shops

- Earn money with each sale

Upload your text at www.GRIN.com and publish for free

Janine Dehn

Analysis "Garden of Love" by William Blake

GRIN Verlag

Bibliografische Information der Deutschen Nationalbibliothek:

Die Deutsche Bibliothek verzeichnet diese Publikation in der Deutschen National-
bibliografie; detaillierte bibliografische Daten sind im Internet über http://dnb.d-
nb.de/ abrufbar.

Dieses Werk sowie alle darin enthaltenen einzelnen Beiträge und Abbildungen
sind urheberrechtlich geschützt. Jede Verwertung, die nicht ausdrücklich vom
Urheberrechtsschutz zugelassen ist, bedarf der vorherigen Zustimmung des Verla-
ges. Das gilt insbesondere für Vervielfältigungen, Bearbeitungen, Übersetzungen,
Mikroverfilmungen, Auswertungen durch Datenbanken und für die Einspeicherung
und Verarbeitung in elektronische Systeme. Alle Rechte, auch die des auszugsweisen
Nachdrucks, der fotomechanischen Wiedergabe (einschließlich Mikrokopie) sowie
der Auswertung durch Datenbanken oder ähnliche Einrichtungen, vorbehalten.

Imprint:

Copyright © 2006 GRIN Verlag GmbH
Druck und Bindung: Books on Demand GmbH, Norderstedt Germany
ISBN: 978-3-640-31679-3

This book at GRIN:

http://www.grin.com/en/e-book/125685/analysis-garden-of-love-by-william-blake

GRIN - Your knowledge has value

Der GRIN Verlag publiziert seit 1998 wissenschaftliche Arbeiten von Studenten, Hochschullehrern und anderen Akademikern als eBook und gedrucktes Buch. Die Verlagswebsite www.grin.com ist die ideale Plattform zur Veröffentlichung von Hausarbeiten, Abschlussarbeiten, wissenschaftlichen Aufsätzen, Dissertationen und Fachbüchern.

Visit us on the internet:

http://www.grin.com/

http://www.facebook.com/grincom

http://www.twitter.com/grin_com

PS "British Poetry since Romanticism"

LN Literaturwissenschaft

Summerterm 2006

Institut für Anglistik und Amerikanistik

„*The Garden of Love*"

by

William Blake

Janine Dehn

LG Englisch/ Biologie

Staatsexamen

4. Fachsemester

"The Garden of Love"

by

William Blake

I went to the Garden of Love,
And I saw what I never had seen;
A Chapel was built in the midst,
Where I used to play on the green.

And the gates of this Chapel were shut,
And "Thou shalt not." writ over the door;
So I turned to the Garden of Love,
That so many sweet flowers bore.

And I saw it was filled with graves,
And tomb-stones where flowers should be;
And Priests in black gowns were walking their rounds,
And binding with briars, my joys & desires.

„Both read the Bible day and night;
but you read black where I read white." William Blake[1]

I'd like to start my analysis of William Blake's "The Garden of Love" with those lines by William Blake. He refers to the way he's reading the bible compared to the way the church is interpreting it. I think that this quotation reflects the contradictions and ambiguous relations between William Blake and the Church of England. Or rather the way the Church of England was interpreting the Bible and how they wanted the Bible to be read and comprehended by common people. This is connected to the poem, which is a criticizing the Church of England. "The Garden of Love" was published in 1794 as part of the "Songs of Experience".

The special idea of the poem is a lyrical I that is walking around a special garden, which is the "Garden of Love". The lyrical I discovers that the garden has changed. There used to be flowers in the garden. But they are gone and instead the lyrical I finds itself confronted with a chapel that was built in the garden. Furthermore, there are graves, tomb-stones and priests in the "Garden of Love".

The poem creates a feeling of anger and dismay about the changes in the garden. The lyrical I is dismayed about the changes and because its wishes and desires will remain unfulfilled. What's next is that the beauty of the "Garden of Love" faded away through the change. It is accusing the priests and the chapel of being responsible for his unfulfilled wishes because they are "binding with briars" his "joys & desires".

There is a structure in the poem regarding the thoughts and feelings of the lyrical I. In the first stanza the lyrical I describes its wandering through the garden and the changes that it discovers, meaning a chapel where it used to play. This stanza is quiet and gives no hint on negative feelings or thoughts due to the change. In the second stanza it describes the situation in the garden. Its said that the gates of the chapel are shut. There is an inscription above the gates with a general prohibition addressing all mankind. The lyrical I is turning its attention towards the beautiful garden. In the third stanza the lyrical I is describing the garden. Its naming the changes in the garden, the graves, tomb-stones and priests. The lyrical I is disappointed by the changes.

---

[1] Hoeller, Stephan. The Genesis Factor.

The lines are getting more and more emotional, energetic and aggressive throughout the poem. The first stanza is describing a peaceful and idyllic scene. There is no tendency towards aggressiveness and tension yet. But at the beginning of the second stanza there is a turn. The poem is getting more and more negative. There is a contradiction between the peaceful garden scene and the chapel with its closed gates and the inscription. There is a certain tension rising in those lines. The last two lines of the second stanza are again emphasizing the idyllic character of the garden. But in the last stanza the tension is at its highest level. It seems to be harsh and energetic. The words used are containing harder sounds, like in "grave", "priests", "black gowns", "briars" etc. Those voiced and voiceless stops are making the words sound not soft, but rather spitted out with energy. Those lines are full of energy and disapproval. There is a connection between the formal structure and the emotions expressed by certain lines. All lines that are transporting a negative feeling of disapproval or dismay are beginning with the word "And". In the first line there is already the first glance of dismay when it says "And I saw what I never had seen". In this context it sounds rather insignificant, but in relation with the following lines it is clear that here we can find a first contradiction to the idyllic garden scene. It's slowly getting more and more obvious that something has changed in the garden.

The lyrical I does clearly detest the changes in the Garden of Love. It is referring to the church and expressing its dislike. Those lines represent a clear critique addressed to the church and their practices regarding religious beliefs. What's even more, is that the lyrical I accuses the church of "binding with briars my joys & desires", meaning not allowing the lyrical I to be happy but rather putting pressure on it. Compared to the reality in 18th century England, the doctrines and practices of the Church of England, this might express how those felt who did not follow the Church of England and did not agree with their way of interpreting the Bible. It is a provocation and thus still reflecting a part of reality in the 18th century.

The poem consists of three stanzas with each 4 lines, meaning three quatrains. There is no consistent end rhyme scheme. Only two end rhymes are used. In the first and second stanza, lines two and four rhyme (seen – green / door – bore). But Blake in making use of a couple of internal rhymes. In the second stanza, lines one and two, an internal rhyme occurs in "shut" and "not". In the last stanza its "gowns" and "rounds", as well as "briars" and "desires". The meter of the poem is not consistent. The first stanza starts with a regular, harmonious amphibrach. In the second stanza, there is a change in the meter. Blake is here making use of an anapaest, but it still sounds harmonious. Where as, the last stanza is compared to the previous stanzas a bit disharmonious regarding the meter and the length of the lines. In the first line it is still the anapaest of the previous stanza and then there is a turn. The meter is changed to an amphibrach again. In the first stanza we find a trimeter, which can be found in the second stanza too and at the beginning of the third stanza as well. But in the last two lines of the third stanza Blake is making use of a tetrameter, meaning the lines are longer than the previous ones. The meter is not regular, which means Blake is not using one meter consistently throughout the poem.

In "The Garden of Love" quite a few stylistic devices are used, such as assonances, alliterations or anaphoras. An assonance can be found in the last line of the third stanza. Here the rhyme is within the words "briars" and "desires". Another assonance can be found in the line previous to the assonance just mentioned. It says "gowns" and "rounds". We find alliterations, i.e. 3rd stanza/ 3rd line "were walking" or 2nd stanza/ 3rd line "turned to the". A third alliteration can be found in the last stanza, last line where it says "binding with briars". Furthermore, Blake is making use of a consonance, meaning that only the consonances rhyme. This one can be found in the second stanza, line one "chapel were shut". Another obvious stylistic means is the usage of an anaphora. In all stanzas we find the word "And" at beginning of the lines. In the first stanza "And" is only used once, in line two. In the second stanza we find it in the first two lines at the beginning and in the last stanza every line starts with "And". Blake is furthermore repeating the line "And I saw" at the beginning of two separate lines (1st stanza/2nd line and 3rd stanza/1st line). One can consider the line "...to the Garden of Love", used in line one of the 1st stanza and line three of the 2nd stanza, an epipher, meaning the repetition of words at the end of lines.

The outer structure of the poem represents the enclosed meaning. There is a correspondence between the words, that are sharpening, and the meaning. From the outer structure one can see the development from a neutral speaker to an angry speaker, from idyll to a place less idyllic, from a harmonious meter to a disharmonious meter.

The images Blake is using are mainly the "Garden of Love", the "chapel", "priests in black gowns", as well as the "flowers", "briars", "tomb-stones" and "graves".

The "briar" is a plant belonging to the family of the roses, which means it has small sharp points or thorns. This refers to the crown of thorns that Jesus wore before his crucifixion. It is a means of torture used to flagellate people. The crown of thorns is mentioned in the Bible at three different occasions. According to Matthew (27:29), John (19:2) and Mark (15:17), Roman soldiers commanded by Pilatus have put this crown on Jesus` head while making fun of him and torturing him. It doesn't actually say weather he still wore it upon his crucifixion. Jesus was not only given a mocking crown but even a sceptre made of reed and a red cape, according to the Bible. Those symbols of a king given to Jesus by the people that were later on going to kill him were interpreted as making fun of Jesus. They were even making fun of him by calling him "King of the Jews" (Matthew 27:11, Mark 15:2). It was a symbol of derision or mockery. It might have been a crown, but a bitter crown with thorns. The thorns were torturing and in a way flagellating Jesus. This crown of thorns is the opposite of a traditional crown that represents monarchic power and wealth. Opposing to this, the crown of thorns means that although Jesus was the leader of the Jews and the son of God it is making fun of him and not acknowledging his status. Jesus, his mission to bring his people to their land, to free them from slavery in Egypt and his religious beliefs were not acknowledged and he had to suffer because of this. Understanding the meaning of the briar and seeing the context of Blake's poem it means nothing less than that the lyrical I feels tortured and flagellated by the church, which is made responsible for preventing his happiness. It is as the lyrical I states "binding with briars my joys & desires" with its doctrines, strict rules and exclusive right to determine the "good" religious people from those whose beliefs or methods are heresy. The church at that time, and even today, claims being the only authority to interpret the Bible in the "right" way. They prosecuted and tortured everyone who did not follow their way of interpreting the Bible or were somehow a threat to their power and well-being, just to mention the Huguenots in France or the Inquisition. In the Christian tradition strict rules have always been applied and there has always been usage of hard punishment. Through this the church was always oppressing resistance. All other ways of reading the Bible and interpreting it were damned, just like the Gnostic views that Blake was representing. Blake makes a clear statement against the Church of England, their methods and dogmas through this poem. The lyrical I does clearly detests the changes in the Garden of Love. It even reproaches the chapel and priests for his desires and joys remaining unfulfilled, as I will explain a bit later. It describes a horrible picture of the garden with its graves, priests in black and all flowers vanished. That is a strong statement of rejection, compared to the idyllic and bright descriptions of the previous Garden of Love with its flowers and green playgrounds. Even the name "Garden of Love" is promising something bright and peaceful, a place of happiness. Those words represent a critique on the church and it furthermore even says that the church is restricting and flagellating the people. Just like the Romans did with

Jesus through the crown of thorns. The church does not give people religious freedom in ways of understanding the context of the Bible, but applies rather strict rules and through this is prohibiting happiness, according to Blake.

Another hint on the character of the church is stated in the second stanza by the lyrical I. What we can find here is the inscription above the chapel gates stating "Thou shalt not." which is the general term of prohibition used by the church in the Ten Commandments. Striking is the fact that Blake put a full stop after the line, which is making the statement kind of closed and even stresses the prohibition. It does not leave any room for discussion and seems to be even stricter through this. Again, according to Blake, the church is oppressing the people. He is giving their strongest statement that everyone at his time knew and that is somehow representing the church itself. It says nothing less than that it is preventing religious people from being happy (in terms of being allowed a free will and own thoughts) and even that the Christian doctrines and interpretations of the Bible do only contain prohibitions.

Then there is a whole set of images referring to the church and Christian tradition, namely the chapel, priests, tomb-stones and graves. The chapel, as the place of Christian ceremonies and of worship of God, is mentioned in the first stanza. Chapels have ever since been built to cherish God, as places to be the nearest possible to God, and meant to represent the power and wealth of the church (or the person that had the chapel or cathedral built and donated it to the church). And it was meant to give shelter and be a peaceful place of devotion and thought, especially as this is only a small chapel, rather than a huge cathedral. Reading only the first stanza, it seems to represent silence and peace within the garden. It doesn't yet seem to be an intrusion within the garden. In Romanticism a chapel could even represented transience. But then, in the last stanza those Christian symbols are connected to words that have negative connotations. Here it says "priests in black gowns", "tomb-stones" and "graves" can be found in the "Garden of Love". Priests are traditionally meant to be mediators between the faithful and their God. In the Christian tradition the church never meant to allow people direct communication with God except by praying. They always intended to stand between God and the people to mediate. The church was the exclusive interpreter of the Bible for centuries, at the beginning mainly because priests or monk were the only ones who could read. It had always been about telling people how to read and interpret the Bible. And those "priests in black gowns" are an authority. This image represents the power and authority of the church. It is somehow even creating a feeling of being overpowered by those dark men. The lyrical I is probably being outnumbered because it mentions not only one but a couple of priests. And they are walking through the garden, along further negative symbols, namely the graves and tomb-stones. Those are symbols of hopelessness, death and despair. The black gown is another item evoking a feeling of authority, dignity or even an incredible power and knowledge. Just imagine those priests with all their authority and dignity unexpectedly walking through the "Garden of Love". The garden suddenly loses his peacefulness and brightness that one might have imagined. It gets a dark and threatening touch. Its beauty and promising character is gone, it vanished just like the flowers. The same happened to the "joys & desires" the lyrical I is speaking about now that the priests and the church have taken over possession over the "Garden of Love". All gone. No more playing on the green. No cheerful wandering around. No flowers. No happiness.

Referring to the briars and its use as crown of thorns, I mentioned earlier on that in botanical terms it belongs to the family of the roses. The rose is another Romantic symbol, representing earthly and Christian love. So, there is again a symbol referring to Christ. The lyrical I keeps further on mentioning other flowers in the "Garden of Love". Flowers could represent different things in Romanticism, just to mention the well-known image of "die blaue Blume der Romantik" in German Romanticism. They were symbols with negative or positive connotation, i.e. violets as symbols for humility. Unfortunately, Blake doesn't tell us what kinds of flowers are growing in the garden.

Another most powerful image that Blake uses is the "Garden of Love" itself, a place described as being essential for the lyrical I´s happiness and the fulfilment of his desires. But it gets intruded by "the church" and all his hopes simply fade away, just like the flowers. This garden refers to the biblical Garden in Eden, the place where Adam and Eve as the first human beings created by God lived until the fall of men. In the first book of Moses, chapter two (1:8) it says, God created a garden in a place called Eden and was putting the human (meaning Adam) into this garden. God was creating trees and plants to feed Adam and told him to look after them (2:9, 15). And he had the Tree of Life and the Tree of Knowledge of Good and Evil planted in the Garden. There were four rivers flowing through the garden, one of them the Euphrat (2:10, 14). At the very same place God is creating a companion for Adam (2:18, 19) and they were living peacefully and happily, being supplied with everything they needed. But when eating an apple from the Tree of Knowledge if Good and Evil, the fall of man put an end to their life in the garden. God is driving Adam and Eve out of the Garden in

Eden. God's garden in Eden is commonly equated with the paradise. It is frequently said that Adam and Eve were driven out of the paradise. The church commonly describes the paradise as the Garden of God, meaning the Garden in Eden, a "Lustgarten" or the place where the dead rest. For common believers the Garden Eden equals the heavenly paradise, the place Christians are hoping to be after their death. So, I assume that Blake refers to the Garden Eden as well as the heavenly paradise that good Christians are admitted to after their death if they were living a faithful life according to Christian rules. At that time the Church of England determined who was a good and faithful believer and who wasn't. This again refers to the "Thou shalt not." inscription over the chapel gates. So, the rules and restrictions of the earthly church have entered the biblical paradise. No one will be admitted who doesn't stick to those rules. But through this the garden loses his heavenly character. And even more striking is that symbols of death and hopelessness have entered the heavenly garden. It had been a place where the lyrical I was free to play and seek the fulfilment of his joys and desires, which are as I suppose religious freedom and freedom of thought. But the earthly instruments of religious moral, their doctrines and believes have entered it, meaning the priests etc. Through those symbols of death in the former paradise, it ain´t a paradise anymore. Its paradise-like features have vanished just like the flowers, according to the lyrical I.

So, what we can find here is a clear critique on the religious beliefs represented by the Church of England and the mainstream interpretation of the Bible. Just as Blake said: "...they read black, where I read white."

Blake grew up in a "...dissenting tradition of private devotion and private Bible reading rather than public catechism and public worship."[2] The term dissenter was commonly used for all religious movements that did not agree with the doctrines of the Church of England. It was actually used as a general classification and did not respond to a single group of religious believers. Dissenters in general believed that "...all truth lies in the Bible and that the proper interpreter of that truth is the individual conscience, not the priest or the church."[3] Blake was a deeply religious man. At that time the name for "extreme Dissent...was Enthusiasm"[4] and that was, according to Bentley, what Blake identified himself with[5]. It further on says that "They believed that all institutions, beginning with the Church and the State, were tyrannical

2 Bentley, Gerald E. The Stranger from Paradise: A Biography of William Blake. p. 7
3 Bentley, Gerald E. The Stranger from Paradise: A Biography of William Blake. p. 7
4 Bentley, Gerald E. The Stranger from Paradise: A Biography of William Blake. p. 8
5 Bentley, Gerald E. The Stranger from Paradise: A Biography of William Blake. p. 8

attempts to bind to Satan's Kingdom the souls which Christ had come to free,..."[6] It is not only that they were rejecting the Church of England, in their understanding the church was evil. They were worshiping God in their private houses, were not attending to divine services and frequently interpreting the Bible in other ways than what was approved by the Church of England. So, Blake read the Bible, he actually "read widely and not merely on the religious subjects"[7] and that's what he was inspired by and where his believes derived from. He actually "...studied the literature of the occult and the esoteric..."[8] Blake's beliefs were considered to be heresy and as Bentley points out "...Blake did not read the Bible merely in its literal or its orthodox sense. "He understands by the Bible the Spiritual Sense For as to the nature sense that Voltaire was commissioned by God to expose."[9] Blake was drawing conclusions from the Bible that did not correspond with the doctrines of the Church of England. "The world is ruled by the Beast and the Whore"(meaning the church and the state), Christ was wrong to sacrifice himself for the salvation of man, his strong rejection of the church and public worship or Satan as „father & God of this World" [10]just to name some of Blake's beliefs that were heresy. Throughout his life Blake was searching for spiritual truth and spiritual peace beyond the doctrines of the Church. "For Blake paradise was the human imagination, and he spend most of his life there."[11] There are various stories of visions and apparitions that Blake claimed to have, which is another hint onto his immense imagination and creativity, but even let to speculation about his mental health. The point is that William Blake was a man of deep religious beliefs and outstanding imagination, who was seeking for answers and deeper truth in life. And he found those answers in Gnosticism. Gnostic beliefs and way of reading and its interpretations of the Bible were quite different from the interpretations of the church. And Blake was criticizing the church through his poems. In "The Garden of Love" he is pointing out that the church and their doctrines are responsible for people not being free to think and interpret; for being betrayed from their hopes, joys and desires. The church as an institution is preventing people's happiness, their "joys & desires" through their "briars" and priests. It is restricting the faithful, not allowing own interpretations of the Bible's content and actually finding the deeper truth in it. It is rather centred on keeping their power and wealth alive, on condemning, torturing and flagellating everyone who doesn't agree with their doctrines. This opinion of Blake's derived from the new understanding of the

[6] Bentley, Gerald E. The Stranger from Paradise: A Biography of William Blake. p. 8
[7] Bentley, Gerald E. The Stranger from Paradise: A Biography of William Blake. p. 26
[8] Abrams, M.H. Norton Anthology of English Literature- Volume Two, p. 10
[9] Bentley, Gerald E. The Stranger from Paradise: A Biography of William Blake. p. 9
[10] Bentley, Gerald E. The Stranger from Paradise: A Biography of William Blake. p. 9-11
[11] Bentley, Gerald E. The Stranger from Paradise: A Biography of William Blake. p.xxv

individuality of man and the new spirit that arose in Romanticism. The poem was written at a time of immense changes, the American and the French Revolution, the Industrial Revolution. All that had consequences in society. The change was from an agricultural society to an industrialized society, whose impact on the people was strongly formative. A new working class developed, population grew constantly and demanded more and more food etc. The working and living conditions of those new industrial workers were terrible; they were poor and suffering rather than living. It was a time "...of wars, of economic cycles of inflation and depression, and of the constant threat to the social structure from imported revolutionary ideologies to which the ruling classes responded by heresy hunts and the repression of traditional liberties."[12] For the ruling classes in England, meaning the church and the state, the general enthusiastic support of the French Revolution was a threat to their power and wealth. Many poets supported the ideas of the French Revolution ("Liberté-Egalité-Fraternité"), the individuality of man and the new way of thinking. At the beginning, they were inspired by it, but just alike Blake, they soon dropped it when the French Revolution turned out to be violent (Reign of Terror under Robespierre, Napoleonic Wars) and their hopes were betrayed. Actually, "In England this period was one of harsh repressive measures."[13] Perhaps the increasing oppression was another reason for Blake's harsh critique, to sort of write against the increasing oppression of its time. At the beginning, people felt the French Revolution was "a time of promise, a renewal of the World"[14] As this statement by Wordsworth points out, there were incredible hopes related to the French Revolution and the new ideologies rising in France. They felt it a time of "limitless possibilities"[15] "...not only in the political and social realm but in intellectual and literary enterprises as well."[16] The status of the poet itself as an artist was newly defined, a new self-confidence and individuality developed. The new status not only of artist, but of the individual itself derived from the "...rejection by philosophers of a central eighteenth-century concept of the mind as a mirrorlike recipient of a universe already created, and its replacement by the new concept of the mind as itself the creator of the universe it perceives."[17] Humans had so fare been understood and seen as "limited beings"[18], but now people were beginning to see their potential, possibilities and power. There was a new importance and emphasise on feelings, emotions and thoughts. Artists felt chosen and

---

[12] Abrams, M.H. Norton Anthology of English Literature- Volume Two, p. 1
[13] Abrams, M.H. Norton Anthology of English Literature- Volume Two, p. 2
[14] Abrams, M.H. Norton Anthology of English Literature- Volume Two, p. 4
[15] Abrams, M.H. Norton Anthology of English Literature- Volume Two, p. 4
[16] Abrams, M.H. Norton Anthology of English Literature- Volume Two, p. 4
[17] Abrams, M.H. Norton Anthology of English Literature- Volume Two, p. 10
[18] Abrams, M.H. Norton Anthology of English Literature- Volume Two, p. 10

inspired. "Blake insisted that he wrote from "Inspiration and Vision"[19]. And what's so striking about Blake is, that he was writing "...a symbolist poetry in which a rose, a sunflower,...is represented as an object imbued with a significance beyond itself."[20] In Romantic poetry we can frequently find descriptions of landscapes and there was a general emphasise on nature. But, "Romantic poems habitually endow the landscape with human life, passion, and expressiveness."[21] So, the garden can not be understood as merely a garden. Actually, "...by Blake mere nature, as perceived by the physical eye and unhumanized by the imagination, was spurned..."[22] The garden can be understood as a metaphor relating to the paradise or God's garden in Eden, but one could even understand it as something within the Christian believer, it's inner religious "landscape". This individual understanding of religiosity, religious freedom and self-fulfillment that gets intruded or is interfered with by the outer institutions of church and state.

According to this "the emphasis in this period on the free activity of the imagination is related to an insistence on the essential role of instinct, intuition, and the feelings of "the heart" to supplement the judgement of the purely logical faculty, "the head"..."[23]. Feelings are emphasized rather than rationality. Romanticism was even a period not only of thought, but to a certain extend even of melancholy. Perhaps, a bit of this melancholy can be found in the mood of the speaker, in the vanished peace and flowers. But there is an even stronger tone of anger developing throughout the lines of the poem. As I said, the poem is part of the "Songs of Experience", who are the complement to the "Songs of Innocence". Bentley describes the "Songs of Experience" as "...songs of the unprotected, songs of betrayal or at least a sense of betrayal, the laments of the victims. They are cries of honest indignation and social protest..."[24]

I think, considering all the images, their meaning, the facts known about William Blake's life, his opinion about religion and the mood of the Romantic period; all is embodied in this critical poem.

[19] Abrams, M.H. Norton Anthology of English Literature- Volume Two, p. 6
[20] Abrams, M.H. Norton Anthology of English Literature- Volume Two, p. 8
[21] Abrams, M.H. Norton Anthology of English Literature- Volume Two, p. 7
[22] Abrams, M.H. Norton Anthology of English Literature- Volume Two, p. 8
[23] Abrams, M.H. Norton Anthology of English Literature- Volume Two, p. 7
[24] Bentley, Gerald E. The Stranger from Paradise: A Biography of William Blake. p. 144

I'd like to finish my observations on "The Garden of Love" with another quotation by William Blake.

"The Nature of my Work is Visionary or Imaginative."[25]

---

[25] Abrams, M.H. Norton Anthology of English Literature- Volume Two, p. 19

Works cited:

Abrams, Meyer Howard. The Norton Anthology of English Literature-Volume Two. New
York: Norton. 1993.

Bentley, Gerald E. The Stranger from Paradise: A Biography of William Blake. New Haven:
Yales University Press. 2003.

Gilchrist, Alexander. Gilchrist on Blake Life of William Blake. London: Harper Perennial.
2005.

Hoeller, Stephan A.The Genesis Factor. 05 May 2006. <http://www.webcom.com/gnosis/>

Kazlev, Alan. The Kheper Homepage. Gnosticism. 10 June 2006.
<http://www.kheper.net/topics/Gnosticism/intro.htm>

Moore, Edward. Gnosticism. The Internet Encyclopedia of Philosophy. 10 June 2006
<http://www.iep.utm.edu/g/gnostic.htm>

Robinson, B.A. Ontario Consultants on Religious Tolerance. Religious Tolerance.org.
Gnosticism: Ancient and Modern. 10 May 2006
<http://www.religioustolerance.org/gnostic.htm>